BUILDING THE WORLD

ENGINEERING

PAUL MASON

WAYLAND
www.waylandbooks.co.uk

First published in Great Britain
in 2019 by Wayland
Copyright © Hodder and Stoughton,
2019

Series editor: Julia Bird
Produced by Tall Tree Ltd
Editor: Jon Richards
Designer: Ed Simkins

HB ISBN: 978 1 5263 1122 1
PB ISBN: 978 1 5263 1121 4

Wayland
An imprint of Hachette Children's Group
Part of Hodder and Stoughton
Carmelite House
50 Victoria Embankment
London EC4Y 0DZ

An Hachette UK Company
www.hachette.co.uk
www.hachettechildrens.co.uk

Printed and bound in China

Picture credits: **Shutterstock:** 1c, 2c, 2tl,
2b, 10cl, 15cr, 18tr, 19, 15b, 22tl, 26t, 27b,
31tr, 32br Macrovector, 1br, 14-15, 15t
Adazhiy Dmytro, 2tr, 7t Great Vector
Elements, 1br, 2cb, 11r 19cr, 18bl, 22-23,
23tr, 23b Golden Sikorka, 4tr Peter Turner
Photography, 4-5 ollirg, 5tr bibiphoto, 6-7
tele52, 8br Michal Stipek, 8-9 beeboys,
10-11 Alexze, 10t Elena Eskevich, 11tr
metamorworks, 12-13 shutterlk, 12br
MicroOne, 16-17 Santi Rodriguez, 1,
18–19, 19br, 31b, 26-27 VectorPot, 20t
Wangkun Jia, 20-21 Songquan Deng, 21t
Leonid Andronov, 22cb vectorpouch,
24-25 Vadim Petrakov, 25t andzher, 25b
Andrew Clifforth, 28-29 curraheeshutter,
29tl waniuszka, 29cr Michael G McKinne,
Creative Commons: 12tl LOC, 16c
Armando Mancini

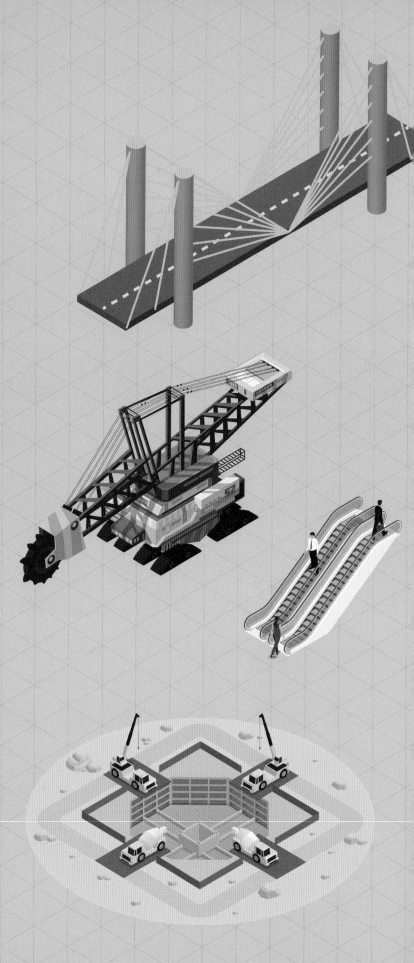

Engineering
EVERYWHERE

Engineering is the design and building of useful things. Without engineers, humans would still be living in caves, wearing animal skins and walking everywhere!

Make it real

Engineers are people who turn ideas into reality. Imagine a group of Stone-Age people standing beside a river, talking about how great it would be to get across. One person finds some big rocks and throws them in the river to walk on, making a bridge. That person is one of the earliest 'engineers'.

The first bridges were simple stone platforms crossing streams.

Big engineering

Today, the biggest, most obvious kinds of engineering are all around us. The road or footpath you travel on, the bus, bike, train or car that carries you, the buildings you pass, and (of course) any bridges you cross – all of them were built by engineers.

Engineering is used to construct towering skyscrapers.

Hidden engineering

Behind big engineering projects are other kinds of engineering that might not be so obvious. Anything made of metal, for example, could not exist without mining engineers. They help to plan and create the mines that provide raw materials for making metal, while vehicle engineers build the huge excavating machines that dig out the raw material, as well as the giant trucks that carry it away.

Giant excavating machines churn up the earth with great force.

One survey estimated that **23% of the UK's total earnings** come from **engineering.**

Engineering changes

The things engineers can achieve are changing all the time. The materials they use are constantly getting better. A hundred years ago, for example, steel and concrete were not as strong as today. This affected what engineers could build and structures had to be smaller. Today, engineers can also use computer programs while working on projects, such as the 'smart' road on page 23.

Building
BRIDGES

Until 200 years ago, people who wanted to cross wide rivers, estuaries or deep gaps in the terrain usually had to either catch a boat or find somewhere easier to cross. Then engineer James Finley invented the suspension bridge in 1801.

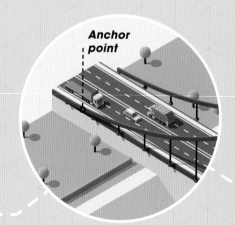

Suspension bridges

A suspension bridge is a type of bridge with a roadway that is suspended from two or more strong metal cables. These cables are strung from two tall towers called pylons.

Anchor points

At either side of the body of water are anchor points for the main cables. These must be dug in securely so they can't move.

Pylons

The pylons support the main cables and the weight of everything that hangs from them. When crossing water, the pylons rest on artificial 'islands'.

Pylon ---

Island

Anchor point

Cable-stayed bridges

These are similar to suspension bridges. Instead of having a main cable, all the suspender cables come from the top of the pylons.

Cable-stayed bridge

Steel cables

The main cables are usually made of tough steel. They are anchored to each side of the river and the tops of the pylons.

Main cables

Suspended roadway

Hanging down from the main cables are lighter 'suspender' cables. These hold up the roadway.

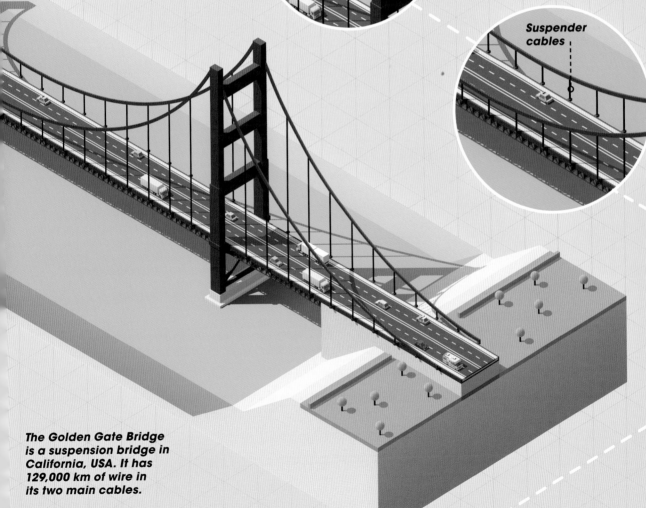

Suspender cables

The Golden Gate Bridge is a suspension bridge in California, USA. It has 129,000 km of wire in its two main cables.

Extreme
BRIDGES

New technology means engineers can build bridges connecting gaps that would have seemed impossible to cross 50 years ago.

The longest bridge?

There is no agreed way to measure a bridge. Some super-long bridges are actually partly causeways (raised roads or tracks). The world's longest suspension bridge is the Akashi Kaikyō Bridge in Japan. Its central span is about 1.93 kilometres from pylon to pylon.

The Charles Kuonen Suspension Bridge has 8 tonnes of cables.

The longest footbridge

At 494 metres from end to end, the Charles Kuonen Suspension Bridge in the Swiss Alps is longer than the distance around an Olympic athletics track. At its highest, the bridge is eight-and-a-half times taller than the highest Olympic diving board (85 metres).

Sydney Harbour Bridge in Australia was built using **6 million metal rivets.** Its arch weighs **39,000 tonnes** and **rises or falls up to 18 cm** with changes in temperature, as the steel it is made from expands or contracts.

The oldest bridge

In the city of Izmir, Turkey, a single-arch bridge crosses the River Meles. The bridge is still used today – despite being almost 3,000 years old. It is thought to have been built in about 850 BCE, making it the oldest bridge still in use.

40 kg

18 cm

The **Duge Bridge** in China has the **longest drop** of any bridge in the world. It towers over **565 metres** above the valley floor below. **A 40 kg weight** dropped from its road deck would hit the ground **10.7 seconds later.**

The Akashi Kaikyō Bridge was built after 168 people died when two ferries sank in the Seto Inland Sea in 1955.

High LIFE

The world's population increases every year, but the world itself cannot get bigger. One engineering solution to this is constructing tall buildings that can fit a lot of people into a small area of land.

Older buildings

These are usually wider and shorter than modern buildings. Before the late 19th century, engineers did not have the advanced steel, concrete and glass technology of today.

Old timber frame building

Foundations

All tall buildings need to be built on a solid base, or there is a risk they will fall down. The foundations are often made of a network of steel beams.

Foundations

The foundations of the tallest buildings may go down to rock, more than 50 metres below the surface.

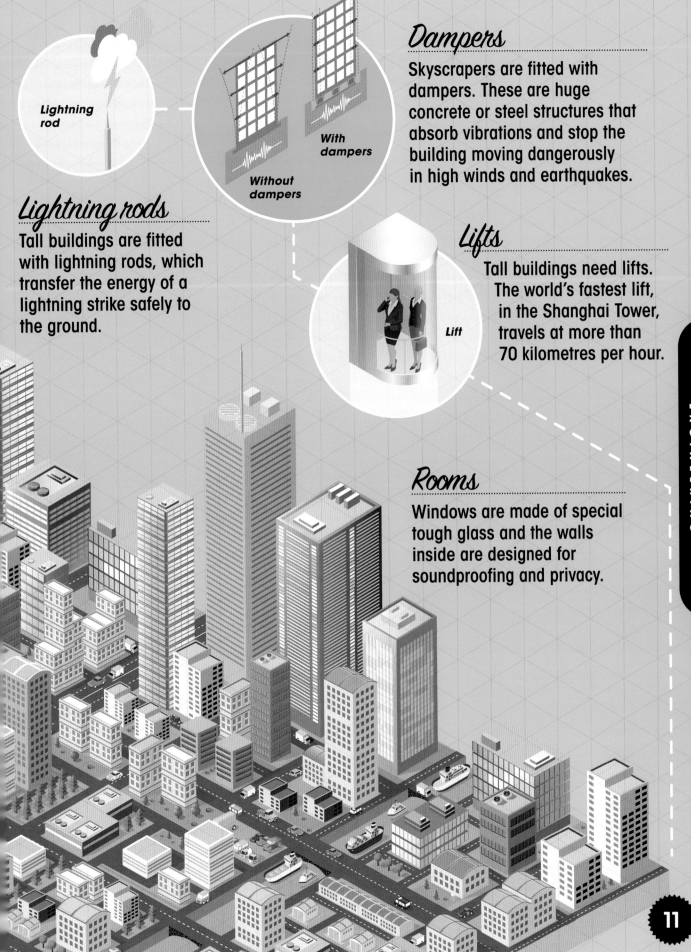

Dampers

Skyscrapers are fitted with dampers. These are huge concrete or steel structures that absorb vibrations and stop the building moving dangerously in high winds and earthquakes.

Lightning rod

With dampers

Without dampers

Lightning rods

Tall buildings are fitted with lightning rods, which transfer the energy of a lightning strike safely to the ground.

Lifts

Tall buildings need lifts. The world's fastest lift, in the Shanghai Tower, travels at more than 70 kilometres per hour.

Lift

Rooms

Windows are made of special tough glass and the walls inside are designed for soundproofing and privacy.

How skyscrapers GREW UP

Until the 1880s, it was impossible to build skyscrapers. This was because as buildings get taller, they get heavier. Back then, the walls at the bottom could not be made strong enough to support a really tall tower.

The Home Insurance Building's architect apparently invented the building's steel frame after seeing his wife rest a heavy book on a small birdcage.

The first skyscraper

In 1885, the Home Insurance Building opened in Chicago, USA. It was revolutionary because it was built around a steel frame and stood 42 metres tall. The frame, rather than the walls, supported the building's weight. Now buildings could go higher than ever before.

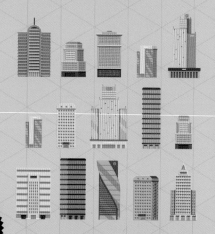

Between *1950* and *2018,* the number of *skyscrapers* that are a) *over 150 m tall* and b) *have more than 40 floors* rose by *8% every year!*

12

Record-breaking skyscrapers

In 1900, the world's tallest building was the Eiffel Tower in France, at 300 metres. By 2010, the record had risen to 828 metres when the Burj Khalifa skyscraper was opened in Dubai. The Burj Khalifa is still the world's tallest building, but some even bigger skyscrapers are being planned.

The Burj Khalifa has more than 160 floors with shops, offices, hotels and apartments.

At **828 metres tall,** the **Burj Khalifa** is the same height as *two Eiffel Towers* standing on top of each other ... **with another three-quarters of an Eiffel Tower on top!**

Monster of the future

In 2021, a building even taller than the Burj Khalifa is due to open. Construction of the Jeddah Tower in Saudi Arabia began in 2013. When the building is finally finished, its tip will be a kilometre from the Earth's surface. The tower uses special concrete and steel to stop the upper parts swaying too much.

When it opens, it is thought the **Jeddah Tower** will have cost **£1.1 million** per **metre** to build.

BURJ KHALIFA

EIFFEL TOWER

Tunnel
TECHNOLOGY

Digging a tunnel is a way of getting under big obstacles, such as mountain ranges, rivers or the sea. Modern tunnels are most often designed to be used by cars, trucks or trains.

ENGINEERING

Today's tunnel-boring machines (TBMs) can dig their way through anything from sandy soil to solid rock.

Cutting head

Disc cutters at the front of the TBM cut into the rock, breaking it into small pieces. The pieces are pushed back through holes in the cutting head.

Hydraulic jacks push the TBM forwards, helping it to cut through the soil or rock.

Waste removal

A conveyor belt carries the pieces of rock away. Waste-removal trucks then carry the material away from the TBM.

Road or rail?

In some tunnels, roads are laid, as well as traffic signals and air systems to remove exhaust fumes. Other tunnels are fitted with train tracks.

A motorway tunnel through a mountain

Finishing touches include power lines and lighting.

Surface connection

Once the tunnel is cut and reinforced, it can be connected to the surface. Emergency exits are added, in case of fire or any other disaster.

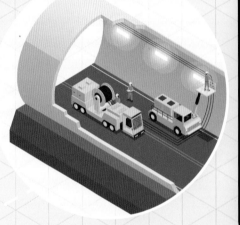

Fitting concrete reinforcements

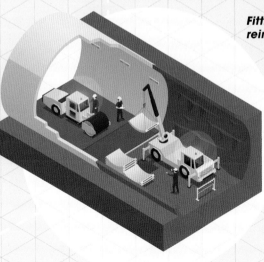

Reinforcements

As the TBM cuts forwards, concrete reinforcement panels are added to the new tunnel to stop it collapsing.

Amazing TUNNELS

In the past, tunnels were usually quite short – partly because they had to be dug by hand. Today's TBMs have made it possible to build some monster tunnels.

Early tunnels

Some of the first tunnels we know about were irrigation tunnels in what is now Iran. Transporting water underground kept it cool in the shade and slowed evaporation. The Ancient Greeks and Romans also built tunnels. In about 36 BCE, the Romans built a tunnel between Naples and Pozzuoli in Italy. Known as the Grotta di Seiano, the tunnel is 770 metres long and 9 metres high.

The Grotta di Seiano was built by a Roman engineer called Cocceius.

The longest tunnels

The world's longest tunnels carry water. The Delaware Aqueduct tunnel in the USA is 137 km long. The three longest tunnels that people can travel through are all rail tunnels.

1 Gotthard Base Tunnel in the Swiss Alps: **57.104 km**

2 Seikan Tunnel under the Tsugaru Strait in Japan: **53.85 km**

3 Channel Tunnel beneath the English Channel: **50.45 km**

Each day in 2018, about **60,000 people** travelled through the **Channel Tunnel.**

The Lærdal Tunnel

The world's longest road tunnel is the 24.5 km Lærdal Tunnel in Norway (below), which opened in 2000. The tunnel is so long that it has:

• three large caves, six kilometres apart, to give drivers a change of scene, a place to rest, and somewhere to turn a large vehicle around if the tunnel ahead is closed.
• emergency phones every 250 metres: whenever one is picked up, signs automatically light up all along the tunnel, saying, *Snu og køyr ut* ('Turn around and leave').
• niches every 500 metres in case of emergencies.
• a special air-filtering system that removes dust and harmful gases from exhaust fumes.

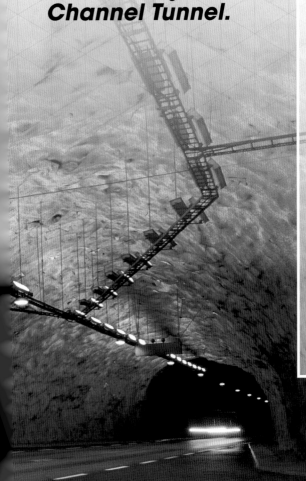

Underground *STATION*

In crowded cities, underground railways – also called subways – are a fast, easy way to move around. The stations for these railways are full of clever engineering.

ENGINEERING

Platform safety

Most new subways use a 'closed' platform system, where there is another wall between the platform and the train. Sliding platform-screen doors open when the train stops, so that passengers can get off and on.

On 'open' platforms, there is no barrier between the platform and the track. It is possible for passengers to fall in front of a train.

STATION

Arrivals and departures board

Announcements

As a train approaches, it triggers an automatic announcement or an update on the digital arrivals screen.

18

Barriers

Barriers

Barriers check passengers' tickets. They can sometimes also take payment from contactless payment cards.

Escalators

Moving staircases help passengers reach street level. To save power, some new escalators only start up when a passenger crosses through a sensor beam.

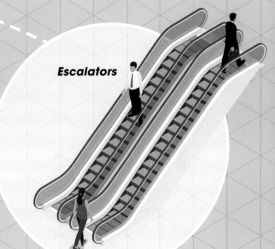
Escalators

Ticket machines

On modern subways, passengers can buy travel tokens or a card loaded with credit, which can be used for several journeys.

Card and tokens

Smoke detector

Fire systems

Fire is a serious risk underground. Stations are fitted with smoke detectors, which can set off alarms.

Subway DEVELOPMENT

The very first subways carried relatively few passengers. Today, technology allows engineers to design subways that carry millions of people a day.

The first subways

The world's first subway system was the London Underground. When it opened on 10 January 1863, the carriages were pulled by steam trains. Boston had North America's first subway in 1897 and the New York City Subway opened in 1904. In South America, the Buenos Aires Subte system opened in 1913.

The Boston Metro (above) makes it easier to travel around the metropolitan area.

On the day the **London Underground** opened in *1863*, more than **30,000 people** travelled on it.

Driverless trains

On many new subway lines, the trains do not have drivers and everything is controlled and monitored by computer. There are systems like this in São Paulo, Toronto, Singapore, Istanbul, Paris and many other cities. For safety, subways with driverless trains almost always have platform-screen doors.

This driverless train operates in Dubai.

3.8 billion journeys were made on the **Beijing subway** in 2017.

Subway record holders

Many subway record-holders are in Asia:
- Shanghai, China, (above) currently has the largest subway system (in 2018 there was 676 km of track), while China's Beijing subway is the busiest
- The shortest subway line is the 4.1 km Minatomirai Line in Yokohama, Japan
- Japan is also home to the biggest station: Ginza, in Tokyo. The station is so large it has 48 entrances!

New
ROADS

New roads are some of today's biggest, most expensive engineering projects. Some of the newest motorways and streets are equipped with 'smart' technology.

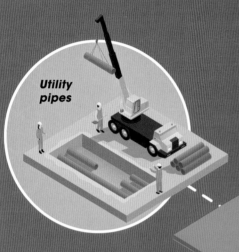

Utility pipes

Utilities

Utilities include water, power and telephone lines. They are buried beneath the road before it is built.

Road construction

First the road's route is cut into the ground. Then the cut is filled with a base, made of quarried rock or gravel. The road surface is laid on top.

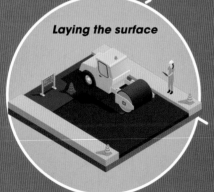

Laying the surface

Most roads have either a slightly flexible top layer or a rigid one. Rigid top layers are usually made up from concrete slabs.

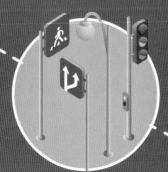

Furniture

'Road furniture', such as traffic lights, signs and safety barriers, is installed last.

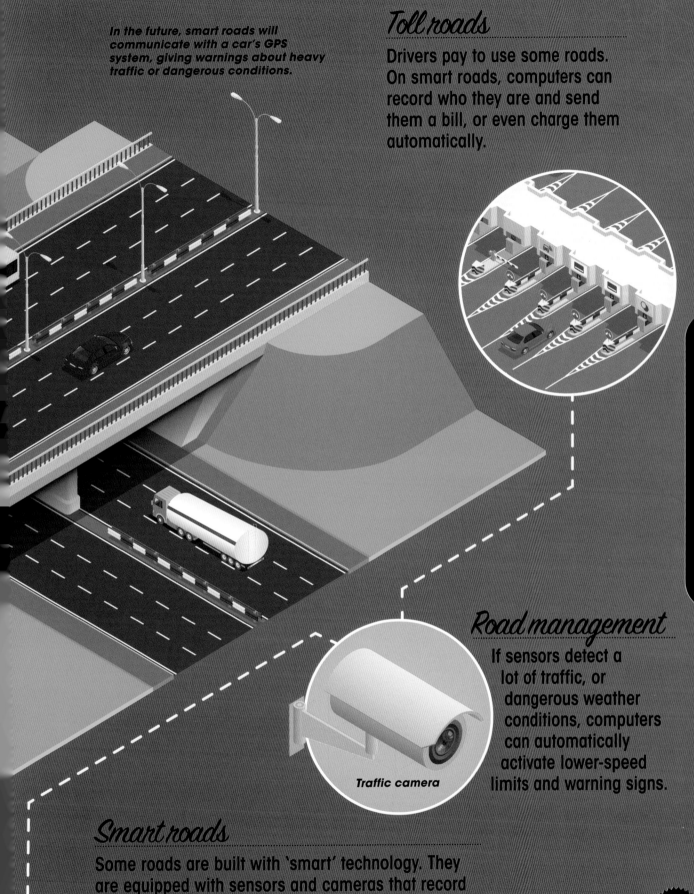

In the future, smart roads will communicate with a car's GPS system, giving warnings about heavy traffic or dangerous conditions.

Toll roads

Drivers pay to use some roads. On smart roads, computers can record who they are and send them a bill, or even charge them automatically.

Road management

If sensors detect a lot of traffic, or dangerous weather conditions, computers can automatically activate lower-speed limits and warning signs.

Traffic camera

Smart roads

Some roads are built with 'smart' technology. They are equipped with sensors and cameras that record traffic, weather and other information.

Extreme ROADS

Long before smart roads had been thought of, engineers were building roads in some amazingly inaccessible places. Here are some of the world's most extreme roads.

Longest road

The Pan-American Highway stretches from Prudhoe Bay in Alaska to Ushuaia in Argentina. Driving down it takes you through the frozen north, tropical rainforests, then back to the freezing southern tip of South America. It is roughly 48,000 km long – more than three times the length of the next longest road, Australia's Highway 1.

In the middle of the Pan-American Highway is the Darien Gap between North and South America. There is no road in this section because the costs are too high.

This photo shows the Pan-American Highway as it travels through the Nazca Desert in Peru.

Coldest road

In the far east of Russia, the Kolyma Highway links the towns of Magadan and Nizhny Bestyakh. Temperatures in the area regularly fall below -50°C in winter. There are fuel stops every 25 km, where drivers have to leave their engines running the whole time. It is so cold that if the engine is turned off, it will not restart.

The Kolyma Highway was built in the 1930s using hand tools. An ambitious feat of engineering, it earned the name 'road of bones' due to the number of people who died building it.

Most dangerous road

The North Yungas Road in Bolivia is believed to be the world's most dangerous. It is also called the *Camino de la Muerte* or 'Road of Death'. The road winds along steep mountainsides, with a sheer drop on one side. It is mostly single-track, with just a few passing places.

The North Yungas road in rural Bolivia.

The **Karakoram Highway** in Pakistan reaches **4,500 metres** above sea level and is sometimes called the **Eighth Wonder of the World.** It is a hazardous route where avalanches and storms are common.

Mined from
THE EARTH

From where you are, can you reach out and touch something metal, or built of concrete? Like many other products we rely on, these are engineered using materials mined from the ground.

ENGINEERING

Open-pit mine

Open-pit mining

Open-pit mines are huge open holes, dug down to remove minerals from the rock. The different levels of the mine are called benches.

The world's deepest open-pit mine is Bingham Canyon in the USA. It is currently 1.2 km deep.

Bench walls

The wall of each bench is angled back to help prevent erosion and rockfalls. (The walls are technically known as 'batters'.)

Angled bench walls

Watery rock

Rock sometimes contains water. Holes are drilled in the walls to let this water out. Otherwise water pressure could crack the wall apart and make it collapse.

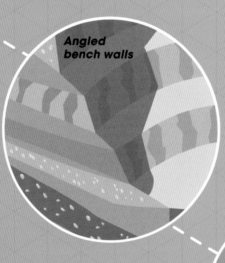

Water contained inside rock

Haul road

Ramps cut into the sides of the mine allow trucks to carry the mined rock out.

Giant trucks

The rock is loaded onto giant trucks, which can carry over 350 tonnes – about 3.5 times the weight of a blue whale.

Explosives are sometimes used to blow the rock apart. The rock is then collected and taken away for processing.

Excavator with cutting drum

Excavating machines

Some excavators use a 'bucket', which is like a giant claw, to break up the rock. Others use a cutting drum, which spins around and chews up the rock.

Deep UNDERGROUND

Some valuable materials are buried too deep to be removed using open-pit mines. Engineers have had to come up with other ways to reach these buried treasures.

Huge oil or gas drilling platforms float in the sea or are fixed to the seabed.

Drilling

Oil and natural gas are usually removed from the earth by drilling. Engineers drill a hole called a well down to the reserve of oil or gas, which then shoots up to the surface. Structures called rigs are built to pipe the oil or gas safely to the surface.

During 2018, **mining engineers** started exploring for **valuable minerals** in more than **2,500** new places around the world.

Deep mines

To reach buried minerals, shafts are dug straight down into the rock. Miners travel down these, then tunnel out sideways in search of the minerals. The heat and dangerous fumes underground mean cool, clean air has to be piped down. Engineers also need to support the mine shaft and tunnels to make sure they do not collapse.

In mountainous areas, miners can sometimes tunnel in from the side of a mountain without digging a deep shaft first.

Fracking

Some underground rocks hold tiny reserves of natural gas. Fracking is a way of removing these. A mixture of water, sand and chemicals is injected into a well at very high pressure. The rock around the well cracks, releasing the gas trapped inside and letting it rise to the surface.

Some people object to fracking. They say it puts harmful chemicals into drinking water and can cause earthquakes.

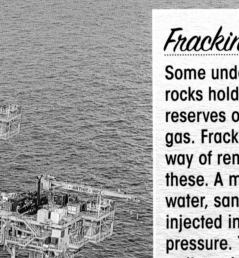

Engineering
WORDS

BEAM
A long piece of metal, wood or another strong material, used to strengthen a building or structure.

CENTRAL SPAN
The middle part of a bridge, where it crosses a river or gap.

CREDIT
On a travel card, credit is money that has been paid to the card and is now recorded on it. The card can now be used to pay for journeys.

DEMOLISHED
Knocked down or taken apart.

EROSION
Wearing away. For example, waves wear away cliffs as they break against them, rivers erode riverbanks and the wind erodes soft rock.

ESTUARY
The place where a river meets the sea and salt water mixes with the fresh river water. Rivers usually widen out at the estuary and may split into more than one branch.

EVACUATE
To leave because danger threatens.

EVAPORATION
The process of water turning into water vapour, which rises into the air.

FRACKING
A method of extracting oil or gas from a rock by pumping a mixture of water, chemicals and sand into the rock.

GPS
Short for Global Positioning System, which uses satellites and radio signals for navigation anywhere on Earth.

IRRIGATION
Use of extra water to help crops grow.

MINERALS
Substances that occur naturally in rocks and earth. Minerals include metals, such as iron and tin, as well as salt and sulphur.

NICHE
A small, shallow opening in a wall.

ORE
A solid material (usually rock) containing valuable metal or some other material that can be separated out and sold.

PRESSURE
The force pushing against a particular area. For example, if someone pokes you in the chest, you feel pressure from their fingertip.

PYLON
A tall structure like a tower or stretched-up pyramid, usually made of a framework of beams.

RESERVE
A store or supply of something.

SENSOR
A device that measures physical things. For example, a moisture sensor measures the amount of water in the air – on a smart road, this could trigger skid warnings.

SINGLE-TRACK
A track that is wide enough for one vehicle.

STRAIT
A narrow channel of water that links two seas or oceans. For example, the Strait of Gibraltar links the Mediterranean Sea with the Atlantic Ocean.

Finding out more

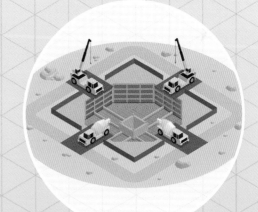

PLACES TO VISIT

SCIENCE AND INDUSTRY MUSEUM
LIVERPOOL ROAD
MANCHESTER
M3 4FP
Open every day, the museum has exhibits about the engineering of railroads, steam engines, flight, cotton production and much more.
WEBSITE: SCIENCEANDINDUSTRYMUSEUM.ORG.UK

SCIENCE MUSEUM
EXHIBITION RD
SOUTH KENSINGTON
LONDON
SW7 2DD
The Science Museum's line-up of guest exhibits is always changing, but usually contains something to fascinate young engineers. Check details on the museum's website.
WEBSITE: SCIENCEMUSEUM.ORG.UK

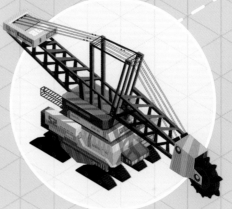

GLASGOW SCIENCE CENTRE
50 PACIFIC QUAY
GLASGOW
G51 1EA
The museum includes an amazing example of what engineering can achieve: the Glasgow Tower. The 127-metre-high tower is the world's tallest free-standing structure that can rotate 360°. When built, it was the only one that could do this.
WEBSITE: GLASGOWSCIENCECENTRE.ORG

WEALD & DOWNLAND LIVING MUSEUM
SINGLETON
CHICHESTER
PO18 0EU
This is a great museum for anyone interested in buildings and how they are built. It features more than 50 old buildings, many of them rescued by being taken apart somewhere else, brought to the museum in pieces and rebuilt in the grounds.
WEBSITE: WEALDDOWN.CO.UK

BOOKS TO READ

CAUSE, EFFECT AND CHAOS IN ENGINEERING AND INDUSTRY
PAUL MASON (Wayland, 2018)
Find out step-by-step not only how some of the world's biggest engineering projects are completed, but also what can go disastrously wrong with them.

THE AWESOME ENGINEERING BOOKS
SALLY SPRAY (Franklin Watts, 2019)
This series of books looks at tunnels, bridges, spacecraft, trains, planes and ships. Using case studies of real-life (and often record-breaking) structures, Sally shows how engineers have constantly pushed forwards the boundaries of what's possible.

Engineering *INDEX*

E N G I N E E R I N G